BREAKING INTO
Butterflies

MIRANDA KULIG

FOR GRANDMA DOROTHY AND MISS CUBBERLY

CONTENTS

To the person holding this book:

if you look through these pages
and see yourself in these words
I promise you are not alone

I do not write *about* people
I write *for* people.

I. Caterpillar

Don't be afraid because you are small, darling
Let me show you where the leaves grow green
and we will dream of wings
that will take us to the sky.

When he first takes your hand
and presses his lips to your knuckles

you may feel butterflies blossom to life
within your chest

but if those butterflies overstay their welcome
and their fluttering wings turn from excited to anxious

listen to them.

At first
I wanted to dive into your pupils
and search the stars that swam there
until every hidden piece of you
was twinkling for me.

I wanted to know
e v e r y t h i n g

You're beautiful
whispered your lips
your eyes
your smile

they say compliments are the quickest way to a girl's
heart
and they were unfortunately right

You knew just the right words
to make my soul

l
    a
       u
          g
            h

Do you remember the night
you walked me to my car?

Laughter echoed down the empty streets of ice and
snow
and our breath swirled in the air above our heads
and nerves prickled across my skin in anticipation for
what I knew was coming next

The butterflies fluttered to life as we stood there in
silent stillness—waiting
uncertainty lingering in the air and falling around our
shoulders like the snow

But when my eyes fell to your lips
and we finally connected
the butterflies in my stomach instantly stopped their
fluttering

and I smiled.

*At the time I thought they had just settled but it turns
out you were smothering them*

I fell for the masterpiece of him that I painted in my
mind where he lived as color and light and magic

but when the sun touched my cheek and made me look
once more
I saw that in truth
he had no colors at all.

Sweetness dripped from your text messages like nectar
and honey
and I was so in love with the flavor that I failed to see
that the same sweetness did not drip from your lips.

When we first met
I wanted to dance with the butterflies that fluttered in
my stomach
and as time went on
it never did occur to me
that perhaps the butterflies should not be there.

You made me nervous for a reason

The first time you asked me if I was happy
I said, "Yes"
because I thought I was.

It turns out I thought wrong.

You once told me I was a beautiful writer
and I was stupid enough to think you were talking about
my words
when you had in fact never read them.

Looking back on us now,
I realized very quickly
that there was a creature hiding behind your eyes

I only wish I had known right away
that it was a snake.

If you tell him no
and he asks you why

leave.

boundaries are boundaries

I can still feel your fingers tracing across my skin
You ran your thumb across

    my jaw

        my nose

            my lips

whispering that I was perfect

I should have listened to the butterflies instead.

*They tried to warn me with their constant fluttering
wings.*

When I met your mother
she made it very clear
that the women in your family
are meant to listen
and not question

and though I did not know it at the time
that was the night
I began forming my wings
and dreaming of the sky.

Can't you see I am made of question marks?

The you I met on the first date
had stars for eyes and sincerity in his smile

I don't know what happened to him
but he broke my heart when he left.

And unfortunately, he left far before I did.

Again, you asked me if I was happy
and this time
I should have told the truth that churned and ached
within my chest

But I wanted you to be who I needed you to be
so I said "yes"
as if lying to myself would change you.

It's funny how quickly elation can turn into disgust.

When he takes your hands
and tells you that he adores your perfect smile

do not be afraid
to deeply search
his beautiful eyes

and if you see the shadow of a snake
coiled within his irises
do not ignore the fluttering wings beating rapidly in
your chest

instead

please

turn

away

and

R U N

A word of advice:

Run when you see the red flags, darling
they are there for a reason

You asked me about our future together
and I was so disgusted
by the idea of a house
and a wedding
and a family
with you
forever

That I wanted to force wings to break through my back
so I could fly far, far, far away from you

But instead
I remained a tiny caterpillar
and whispered
"I don't know."

You see, caterpillars aren't very brave

Isn't it funny
that I used to cry at night
because I wanted a hand to hold

But now that I have yours
I cry harder
because it feels like snake skin

If you have to keep promising yourself

over
                        and over

                                      and over

that they will change
and then it will be better
and then you'll be okay

then they aren't the ones changing.

I went from wanting to know everything about you
to wishing I had never met you

They were once your everything
and now you wish they were your nothing.

Dear You,

You tried so hard
to turn things around on me
and make me seem like the problem

But in reality you are your own problem
you search so hard for more
that you miss what you already have

I am sorry that we could not connect

But my body is not a playing field for your fingertips
my mind is not a top for you to spin in circles
my heart is not a balloon for you to inflate and deflate
at your wish
I am not some dainty woman who will listen to your
every command and obey your every whim like your
mother wanted me to be

I am a creator of words and fire
and I am more than you ever deserved.

If they make you feel guilty for saying the things that so
desperately need to be said

they are the ones with the problem
not you

When his fangs came out
for once I did not fear them

I merely saw their sharp gleam as a challenge
and said
"bite me."

*He pushed me to the point of complete indifference and
for the first time in my life I did not care about the
impact the words on my tongue could have on him.*

did   I

why   ever

stay

in

the

first

place?

Day one without you:

Today I woke up
and I could breathe again.

Day two without you:

you make me feel guilty
and you're not even here

His fingerprints left stains on my mind
and I don't know how to erase them.

he is everywhere and nowhere

On the night we ended
I peeled myself back layer by layer
and exposed the truth I had kept so carefully locked
away inside my chest

your anger curled into my thoughts like a snake around
its prey
but when the fangs of your words tried to strike, they
found nothing to grip

the numbness encased me with indifference so deep that
the sharpness of your tongue did not sting
and the relief that flooded my heart when I realized I
was free of you drowned every word you hissed at me
until all I could hear was silence

and while you slunk away into the night on your belly
hissing that I was the one who should be sorry

I looked in the mirror
and realized I had just shed my very first skin.

Another word of advice:

When you run away
keep running
and don't ever look back.

BREAKING INTO BUTTERFLIES

MIRANDA KULIG

II. Molting

Don't be afraid to shed your skin, darling
Sometimes we must search ourselves
until we are bare
before we can fly.

I have never been
the biggest fan of change

but after it ended
and I shed my skin

I looked in the mirror
and did not recognize the girl staring back at me.

So perhaps now is a good time
to dive into my own pupils
and search my own stars
for who I want to be.

If I don't know myself, I must meet her

That's just it, I think
We must shed these layers of dead skin
in order to become light enough
for our wings to bear us.

The only problem is
that shedding can hurt

and I
like so many people on this earth

am afraid of pain.

So to find ourselves
in this world of unknowns
we must take that fear
and use it as fuel

With growing comes pain
but we have to believe
that the pain is worth it.

because it has to be.

We all look at each other
and see masterpieces

and then we look at ourselves
and we find a flaw on every inch of our skin

so tell me
why is it considered normal
to find beauty in every single thing we see
except for our reflection?

In the mirror stands a girl who looks like me
she tugs at her shirt and hides beneath fabric in hopes to
trick her eyes into seeing something different while the
scale calls to her from the bathroom floor and whispers
lies into her ears

Come and see, come and see
Maybe the number will be one you like this time
Come and see, come and see

And like a fool, she listens
she steps onto the scale
and allows the numbers to break her.

Every. single. time.

You paint such a flawless portrait of perfection
that sometimes I wonder about the secrets you hide
behind your paintbrush.

I would also like to know
why it is considered normal
to look at our children

and when they are just getting a taste
of what the real world holds

we blow out their 18th candle
call them an adult
and proceed to constantly ask them questions
about this brand new life they now have

never stopping for a second
to acknowledge the fear drowning out the joy in their
eyes.

why is it okay for young adults to be terrified of the
future
why is that normal

What a terrible thing it is
to be afraid of the world that we live in.

What do you want to do? they ask us

Everything, we respond

And they laugh
and we just let them laugh
as if we didn't mean what we said.

Here I crawl across the ground like a caterpillar
searching for food
When life stretches my skin and tugs it from my body

It's time to grow
she tells me
It's nearly time to fly

But I gather up this dying skin and try to put it back
into place

Not now
I hiss in reply
I'm afraid of heights.

My biggest fear is that
I will spend so long
searching for
the other
h
a
l
f
of my hea
rt that I won't
even realize that for
ever has come and gone.

"What do you want to do with your life?"

~~Do not ask me that question. I am young. I am learning. I should not have that answer yet. I want to run my fingers across the dirt of every state and travel so far that when I look up I see a sky of new stars. I want to breathe the air of new places and soak in the cultures that swim in this vast planet we call home. I want to pour my soul onto paper and write until my fingers are sore and my mind is numb and a masterpiece is sitting before me. I want to paint the sky with one paintbrush and mix the colors until I create new ones. I want to look in the mirror and love what I see despite the numbers on the scale and the bodies of the other girls around me. I want to rest my head on the shoulder of someone who loves me and doesn't have snakeskin and monster eyes. I want to search every hidden corner of the earth until I find the scattered pieces of my soul and glue them together to form the girl I see staring back in the mirror. I want to **live**.~~

"I'm not sure yet. Just figuring it out."

We are so quick to judge others
that we forget they are human, too

we are all made of the same stardust

You look in the mirror and sadness cracks to life in
your eyes like shards of broken glass
I try to tell you what you see is wrong
but you don't believe a word I say
and that breaks my heart more than I could ever
describe in this short simple poem.

And yet I, too, want to hide under fabric
and use my sweater to cover the parts of me that make
my cheeks burn red

If I avoid the mirror
perhaps I will fool my mind into believing that I am
thin

So I pull my clothes over my head and let the layers
create a boundary between skin and judging eyes
because if they cannot see me, they cannot judge me

So I will hide
like a turtle lost within it shell

the only difference is mine doesn't feel like home

I wonder how many poems are lost at sea inside my mind.

I wonder how many poems are lost at sea inside *your* mind.

Uncertainty and I are best friends
he takes my hand and drags me through each day
Never ceasing to ask what and why and when and how

and when I don't have the answers
he shakes my shoulders and screams that I should

and the sad part is
that I believe him.

Anxiety is that annoying friend that shows up to your
house uninvited and without warning
screeching like a fire alarm every time you take a breath

SOMETHING IS WRONG SOMETHING IS WRONG
SOMEWHERE DON'T YOU UNDERSTAND YOU
SHOULD BE PANICKING

why? you ask, *there's nothing wrong*

but Anxiety latches onto your arm and digs its nails into
your skin
and suddenly its fire alarm voice is the only thing you
can hear
and fiery panic beneath your skin is all you can feel

and even when it leaves just as fast as it arrived
Anxiety's ghost lingers
and becomes your shadow.

Today too many things reminded me of you
and those old butterflies began to flutter in warning
within my stomach

I still have yet to calm them down.

It's three months later and you already have another girl
under your arm

and I'm wondering if you are telling her the exact same
things you told to me
if you are asking her what kind of house she would like
to have some day
or how many kids she dreams about
I wonder if you drag your fingers across her skin
and press your lips to her hand
and whisper about how beautiful she is
and push the boundaries she has set in hopes that
perhaps you can entice her to break them all down

but mostly I think about her
and what is running through her head
as she discovers how terribly fast-paced you are

and I wonder
if she will leave as quickly as I did.

I don't like change
I say as life pushes me down a new road

I don't like change
I scream as I dig my heels into the dirt

I don't like change
I sob as my mind doesn't have a chance to process it all

I don't like change
but life keeps running
I don't like change
because that's how life works
I don't like change
and you can either pick up your feet
I don't like change
or be dragged.

There are seasons of life, they tell me
but I am a leaf torn from the branch in fall
being hurled carelessly through the sky by the wind
and yet it is only spring.

I think everyone searches for something
like the caterpillars search for food

We search for love

We search for wealth

We search for time

We search for ourselves

And we grow so used to this constant searching
that in the end
when we discover what we were looking for
we don't recognize it.

I could look in a hundred mirrors a day
and still see something different every time.

Give me your hand
and I will give you all of the compliments
all of the advice
all of the encouragement
all of the ideas
and all of the love that you need

Tell me to look in a mirror
and give the same things to myself
and I will just laugh
and tell you I don't know what to say

because quite honestly
I don't.

*it is much easier to be nice to others than it is to be nice
to ourselves.*

Sometimes the ghost of your touch haunts me
but as time passes
and my soul grows
I shed the skin you once tainted
and dream of wings instead.

You tell me you want to stay a caterpillar
because you are afraid that growing will hurt

But how can you grace the sky with your colors
if you don't form your wings and fly?

Molting, though uncomfortable,
is not the hardest part

the hardest part is breaking yourself down completely
in order to become something new

the hardest part
is facing the night
when you are desperate for the sun

the hardest part
is putting one foot in front of the other
when all you can see is darkness

but I promise you
the light
and the sky
and your wings

are coming soon.

BREAKING INTO BUTTERFLIES

III. *Chrysalis*

Don't be afraid to protect yourself, darling
Some days are harder than others
and your wings need time to grow.

I once read
that when a chrysalis is formed
the caterpillar is broken down
in order to be made new again
I wonder now
is life my chrysalis?

It was you and me in a booth; 11 PM
Intelligence sparkled in your eyes like the lights
reflecting off the half-empty saltshakers listening in on
our conversation

In that moment, you were different
and you smiled
and I fell

and now here I am seven months later
still mourning the fact that who I thought you were in
that moment; on that night
is not the real you at all

and I still struggle to accept that the you I so eloquently
painted in my mind

does not
and will not
ever exist.

It was so different at first

Why is it
when I look in a mirror and feel good about what I see
that my mind instantly yells at me to step on the scale
so I won't feel good anymore?

I don't think my mind will accept anything other than insecurity

One moment you love the image in the mirror and the
next you want it to vanish from existence

One moment you see the rolls of your stomach as
natural and beautiful and the next you want to iron them
away even if it burns

One moment you choose to eat healthy foods of
beautiful colors and the next you are devouring calories
like you've never had the blessing of sugar on your
tongue

One moment you feel okay and stable and comfortable
and the next you are barreling out of control down a
mountain and the rocks are scratching at your skin and
the dirt is stinging your eyes but you cannot stop
because this is what you have trained yourself to do for
so many years

Climb and fall
up and down
lose and gain

This is normal, the voices scream
and we don't have the courage to ask why.

You think you have the world fooled, don't you?
Pretending to smile when you feel nothing.

we believe we are not allowed to have bad days

Things people tell me and the answers I want to give them:

"You are so talented"
So are a lot of people

"You are a beautiful writer"
Yet I can't stand the words that stain this page

"You have plenty of time"
But time is ceaselessly slipping between my fingers

"You shouldn't worry so much"
But I am made of anxiety

"You should love yourself more"
Can't you see I don't know how?

It's nights like these
When the rain pours steadily around the smiles and
echoes of laughter
and I watch as they huddle in each other's arms
swinging back and forth like a pendulum; like a clock,
ticking
reminding me of how fast time passes
how quickly the years slip by
and as they laugh
and love swims in their eyes
I stay silent
but my thoughts scream.

If jealousy were a fire I would be the coal

Sometimes I crave the other half of my heart so badly
that I physically ache

Other times I am so haunted by the ghost of your scales
dragging across my skin that I don't want anyone to
ever touch me again

If you have to tell yourself to want him
if you have to tell yourself to desire his hands on your
skin
and his lips on your temple
and the hush in his voice

if he presses his mouth to yours
and you have to remind yourself to feel something

do
not
stay
a
minute
longer.

Today I drove the roads where we used to meet
and passed houses that resembled yours
and for a few moments I swear I caught the scent of
dust and cinnamon that settled on the old trinkets your
mother displayed in the living room

I could feel that couch beneath me
and your fingers against my skin

I had to fight to shove the ghost of them away as I
turned my attention back to the road

And though I left you and your snake eyes behind a
long time ago
I realize now that you will always be a shadow
lingering after me that will never disappear
even when the sun shines brightest.

If you had been who I thought you were
I would not be aching right now

But you were not who I needed you to be
and there is nothing I can do about that.

why are you writing this book
        why are you writing this book
                why are you writing this book
        why are you writing this book
why are you writing this book
        why are you writing this book
                why are you writing this book
        why are you writing this book
why are you writing this book
        why are you writing this book
                why are you writing this book
        why are you writing this book
why are you writing this book
        why are you writing this book
                why are you writing this book
        why are you writing this book
why are you writing this book
        why are you writing this book
                why are you writing this book
        why are you writing this book
why are you writing this book
        why are you writing this book
                why are you writing this book
        why are you writing this book
why are you writing this book
        why are you writing this book
                why are you writing this book
        why are you writing this book
why are you writing this book

why are you writing this book
            why are you writing this book
why are you writing this book
why are you writing this book
          why are you writing this book
            why are you writing this book
why are you writing this book
why are you writing this book
          why are you writing this book
            why are you writing this book
why are you writing this book
why are you writing this book
          why are you writing this book
            why are you writing this book
why are you writing this book
why are you writing this book
          why are you writing this book
            why are you writing this book
why are you writing this book
why are you writing this book
          why are you writing this book
            why are you writing this book
why are you writing this book
why are you writing this book
          why are you writing this book
            why are you writing this book
why are you writing this book
why are you writing this book
          why are you writing this book
            why are you writing this book
why are you writing this book
why are you writing this book
          why are you writing this book

Starlight burns in your eyes
twinkling like embers as you watch her
your smile softer than the rain that falls outside

and I wonder, just for a moment
how it would feel to have someone love me
like you love her
and I ache.

How lonely must one be
to desire the heartbreak sung about in songs on the
radio
simply because that heartbreak
means there was once love?

It doesn't matter what I do
I can scream my name or whisper it to the faces blank
like wet concrete walls and I still won't be heard
I can offer every inch of my soul on a platter and serve
it to every passing eye and I still won't be seen
I can show you the words that bleed from my heart in
the middle of the night and paint them into a
masterpiece but someone will always be there to tear
my canvas down and put theirs up in place.
There will always be a crowd that gathers for the rest
There will always be faces that take the attention of
passing eyes
There will always be voices drowning out my tired
screams
and I will always be here
alone
and trying.

The delete key is my worst ~~enemy~~ ~~best~~ friend

I have ~~typed~~ rewritten these ~~words~~ sentences ~~thoughts~~
~~a hundred~~ so many times
that I ~~can't~~ don't even know
what ~~I am trying to~~ this poem is supposed to say
anymore
~~I give up~~

No,
I begged the memories in my head
Please not tonight. I just want to sleep.

But they just laughed and used my mind as their movie
screen anyway.

Bring on the popcorn

~~I wanted to dive into your pupils~~
~~and search the stars that swam there~~
~~until every hidden piece of you~~
~~was twinkling for me.~~

now you haunt me

A nightly ritual:

Open Facebook
New relationship
New relationship

Refresh page
and silently beg for relief.

The page loads
Another relationship
"He's a keeper"
"She's all mine"

Refresh
    Loading . . .
        Loading . . .

Their smiles don't vanish
It's all in your face
Young love, young love
Time is slipping, hold on tight—

You should be more like them

They all found someone to love

Why haven't you

What's wrong with you

    Why
        are
            you
                so
                    unwanted?

Like and comment
~~"So jealous of you guys"~~
"So happy for you guys"
Put the phone away
and go to sleep.

Do you have any idea how it feels
to believe that you are nothing
but a walking inconvenience?

It is late and I should be sleeping
but instead you are on my mind
wandering through my thoughts with your nameless
blank face

You drag your fingers along the walls that leave
imprints I cannot erase
And though I want to,
I cannot call your name
because you are still a stranger
that I have yet to meet

So instead I close my eyes and pretend
that we are sitting together
watching the rain as it pours into puddles outside
as we sip at coffee from painted mugs

and I smile because your presence makes me feel warm
and your touch makes me feel alive

and in this world of make believe
it does not matter
that I don't know your name.

Every so often I have a dream that I am trapped on the
passenger side of a car that is racing down a road of
curves and bumps and hills
my seatbelt locks me in place and refuses to let go and
when I try to reach over and climb into the empty
driver's seat my hands just barely miss the steering
wheel as the car lurches and swerves and speeds down
the wrong side of the road

and though I always start awake just before I crash into
anything
as the day begins, and life races by
somehow I still feel like I'm dreaming.

Sometimes I lie awake at night and stare at the empty
ceiling with memories rolling through my mind like an
old movie

Sometimes I remember words left unsaid
or opportunities missed

Sometimes I daydream myself to the point of tears
knowing that the scenarios I come up with will never be
real

Sometimes I wonder if I made the right choice
if we ended things too soon

Sometimes I wonder why I ever met you at all

But then there are other nights
when I'm surrounded by laughter and s'mores by a fire
and when we all look up and the stars stare back

When I am surrounded by a kind of love that makes me
forget about you
and your snake eyes

and I know with beautiful certainty
that soon I will grow my wings
and be just fine.

Sometimes I feel hopeless like a wave professing its
love for the shore
Ceaseless and sincere
but sent away every time

Other times I feel strong and resilient like the sand
Constantly pulled and scattered
but never disappearing

Here is what I have learned:

If you feel trapped
in your cocoon
then
break
free

Today gold is falling from the sky

it bathes my frostbitten fingers in sunlit silk and
awakens the sleeping parts of my soul like a beast
coming alive after hibernation

it melts across the ground and sweetens the air with
rays of honey and the promise of new beginnings that
reach out and take my hand

Wake up, little butterfly,
Spring whispers in blissful birdsong

And her flower petal smile is so radiant
that even the voices in my head grow silent.

Today
as the sun slipped behind the silhouetted trees
God painted a masterpiece across the sky
and I watched.

He is my favorite artist

In the afternoon I went out on the water
and when I looked over, I saw my reflection in the
waves

She smiled back at me
and I realized that without the numbers attached to her
I liked her

and so I think from now on I will try to keep the
numbers away for good.

I am not a slave to the scale

Listen
you were not born to hide yourself away into the night
or wrap the shadows around your wings because you
believe the colors are too bright for those around you to
see

You were not created to be ignored
or hidden
or forgotten

so please don't listen to their lies.

you were not made to keep the colors of your soul
locked away inside.

In the evening I searched for myself in the sunset that
spread across the lake
and as the marbled colors curled their fingers into the
waves
I think I found a piece of her.

her growing wings are quite beautiful

Out here, in the middle of the lake
I sit in the reflection of the sky
The clouds swim with the fish beneath my paddle
and I follow them to the treasures hidden behind the
sun.

It is so easy to forget that true love exists
when you don't have anyone there to remind you

but that does not mean
you will be forgetful forever.

So, then.
If life is my chrysalis
then perhaps I should have hope
that someday soon
I will have wings.

BREAKING INTO BUTTERFLIES

IV. Wings

Don't be afraid to fly, darling
Your wings are meant to carry no one but yourself.

There is nothing more sweet
than hearing your name
and feeling absolutely nothing.

Who were you, again?

How funny it is to think
that all this time
The love I once desperately craved
was surrounding me

Look at your eyes
look at the places they have seen
the moments they have watched
the memories they have captured

You are a living, breathing phenomenon
of incredible strength and bravery

please don't ever forget that

you are not your anxiety
you are not your flaws
you are not your weight
you are not your mistakes
you are not your depression

you
are
not
your
demons.

I know it's hard but repeat after me

It's amazing what can happen
when you release your heart onto paper
instead of your mind

this book is proof

Looking at a butterfly's wings is like reading poetry written by God.

Do not believe the lie
that you must know everything about the world
in order to understand it
and that you must understand it
in order to live properly in it

it is okay
to say "I don't know"
and to ask for help

it is okay
to not have it all figured out

 It is okay
if right now
you do not have the answers
to everything
you wish you had the answers to

with time
and patience
I promise you
they will come

you just have to believe that.

Having wings
does not mean
that darkness will not roll across the sky
and try to trap you in thunder

What it does mean
is that when these storms
inevitably come
you can set your eyes upon the rainclouds
and fly above them.

Sometimes
all you can do
is remind yourself to breathe

and that's okay

You taught me
That romance is not a requirement of being young
or necessary for me to breathe

You taught me that I am not in desperate need of
someone to hold my hand
or offer me their sweatshirt

You taught me that I should not settle
or try to force myself to feel desire

You taught me that I am far stronger than I ever thought
I was
or ever could be

And most importantly
you taught me that I do not need to search for myself
because I am not lost

you just changed me
and made me stronger
to the point that I didn't even recognize
the girl staring back in the mirror

So even though your name leaves a bad taste in my
mouth

Thank you.

Today I tramped through a muddy pumpkin patch and
fell in love with every pumpkin I saw despite their
many imperfections
And I realized that I need to begin looking at people
that way, too.

Don't be ashamed of your youth, darling
or make it easy for them to look down on you
Instead stand and shake the leaves from the trees
and jump in the piles until the sun loses its color

Your smile will be enough to blind them.

So please
stand on the edge of the clouds
and let your heart paint the beauty of your soul across
the canvas of this world

I promise you, lovely
you are not the darkness you feel.

I once looked in the mirror
and detested what I saw
because what I saw
was a reflection of the number on the scale
but now the scale has no meaning
because it does not have power

I do.

The scale does not control me

Do not believe a word
that the scale whispers to you

It breathes lies instead of air
and spreads them to your ears like a sickness

It reaches for your hand with the promise of a smile but
instead turns and tightens its numbers around your
throat

Believe me, it hisses
I know everything about you.

But no
it cannot see into your soul
or smell your beauty like the roses

All it can tell you
is how much pressure gravity is putting on your body

and that
means

n
    o
       t
          h
            i
              n
                g

Tell me:
are you somewhere far away
pressing your feet against the stars as you tiptoe over
galaxies?

Are you lost between the planets?

Are you wandering amongst Orion?

If so please drop the stars into the ocean
and send the waves crashing over my ankles

That way I will know
that you are coming for me.

He's out there somewhere

.

Today I watched
love dance down
the aisle in a
white gown.
And for the
first time in
months I did not
feel the familiar pang
of jealousy slam into my
gut like a rock. Instead I found
myself smiling as I watched the
tears drip down the groom's face and
kiss the ground. Joy overflowed from
his eyes and his smile and instead of hurt
ing and wishing for a love like that I smiled
so big that my cheeks hurt and my eyes filled
with a similar joy because it had been so long sin
ce I'd seen love like that I almost forgot it existed.

That's the most beautiful part about life, I think.
It never ceases to change.

Don't let the darkness frighten you, dear
The stars will take your hand until the sun can kiss your
cheeks in the morning.

You are so much braver than you believe

I like caterpillars
because if they have the capability
to shed their old skin
and become something new
then perhaps people can, too.

How does it feel
to have the wind rushing across your skin as you bare
your back to the sky?
All this time you thought flying was impossible

Look at you now.

~~why are you writing this book~~
~~why are you writing this book~~
~~why are you writing this book~~
~~why are you writing this book~~
~~why are you writing this book~~
~~why are you writing this book~~
~~why are you writing this book~~
~~why are you writing this book~~
~~why are you writing this book~~
~~why are you writing this book~~
~~why are you writing this book~~
~~why are you writing this book~~
~~why are you writing this book~~
~~why are you writing this book~~
~~why are you writing this book~~
~~why are you writing this book~~
~~why are you writing this book~~
~~why are you writing this book~~
~~why are you writing this book~~
~~why are you writing this book~~
~~why are you writing this book~~
~~why are you writing this book~~
~~why are you writing this book~~
~~why are you writing this book~~
~~why are you writing this book~~
~~why are you writing this book~~
~~why are you writing this book~~
~~why are you writing this book~~
~~why are you writing this book~~
~~why are you writing this book~~
~~why are you writing this book~~
~~why are you writing this book~~
~~why are you writing this book~~
~~why are you writing this book~~
~~why are you writing this book~~
~~why are you writing this book~~
~~why are you writing this book~~
~~why are you writing this book~~

~~why are you writing this book~~
        ~~why are you writing this book~~
                ~~why are you writing this book~~
        ~~why are you writing this book~~
~~why are you writing this book~~
        ~~why are you writing this book~~
                ~~why are you writing this book~~
        ~~why are you writing this book~~
~~why are you writing this book~~
        ~~why are you writing this book~~
                ~~why are you writing this book~~
        ~~why are you writing this book~~
~~why are you writing this book~~
        ~~why are you writing this book~~
                ~~why are you writing this book~~
        ~~why are you writing this book~~
~~why are you writing this book~~
        ~~why are you writing this book~~
                ~~why are you writing this book~~
        ~~why are you writing this book~~
~~why are you writing this book~~
        ~~why are you writing this book~~
                ~~why are you writing this book~~
        ~~why are you writing this book~~
~~why are you writing this book~~
        ~~why are you writing this book~~
                ~~why are you writing this book~~
        ~~why are you writing this book~~
~~why are you writing this book~~
        ~~why are you writing this book~~

I did not choose to write it
the words bled through my fingertips.

Life cocoons me in chaos
and suffocates me in sorrow

But watch out, darling
for in time I will break into butterflies
with wings strong enough to shatter the sky.

BREAKING INTO BUTTERFLIES

ACKNOWLEDGMENTS

First, I would like to thank God. Without Him, I would be nothing.

Thank you to everyone who supported me during the times this collection covers. Thank you to my parents, who have always believed in me as a writer and have always given me the encouragement needed to do what I love.

Thank you to Donna Cubberly—my fourth grade teacher who gave me my first chance at becoming a poet by entering one of my poems into a contest. Thank you for believing in me as a writer even at such a young age. I am sad you are not here to read this book, but I will keep you in my heart always.

Thank you to my Grandma Dorothy, who never fails to encourage me and believe in me. Your beautiful poetry was some of my first inspiration.

Thank you to Mrs. Falk for giving me the courage and desire to turn my ideas into books and collections. Without you, these words would not be here. Thank you also to Maxine Gibson, who furthered that encouragement in college and allowed me to see poetry in a brand new light. Had I not taken your class and learned such wonderful things from you, I am certain this collection would never have been written. In fact, I am certain I would not be writing poetry at all.

Thank you to my sister Kristin and my cousin Cassidy for supporting me from the start and reading the multiple drafts of this collection! Your love and encouragement is what inspired me to publish and share my poetry, and this book would never have been created without either of you.

Thank you to my childhood friend, Alissa, for our dinner dates at Coney Island, hours in the Target book section, and for sitting in my car for hours on end reading each other's poetry. You were one of the first people to read this book and you are one of the reasons it was written.

To all of my followers, thank you for supporting me—whether it has been recently or from the start. You all have such special places in my heart and I treasure each and every one of you.

I also want to thank the men who inspired a lot of these poems. Though our lives were not meant to be intertwined, our time together taught me things that have made me into a stronger person. And, you make a good muse.

Lastly, I want to thank whoever is holding this book and reading these words right now. Thank you for supporting my dreams and reading this small portion of my heart. You are one of the many reasons I write and share my love of poetry with the world, and you mean more to me than I could ever describe in words. Thank you from the bottom of my heart.

Miranda

ABOUT THE AUTHOR

Miranda Kulig picked up a pencil at the age of six and has had a hard time putting it down ever since. She is a writer of poetry as well as fiction and has been previously published in the *Huron River Review* (issue 15), *Michigan's Best Emerging Poets,* and *America's Best Emerging Poets.*

When she isn't writing, Miranda can be found cuddling adorable babies, drinking Starbucks at Target, watching sunsets by the lake, or working on her next book.

To learn more about Miranda and her writing, please visit www.mirandakwrites.com

You can also find Miranda on any of her social media profiles:

@miranda_kulig

@mirandakuligauthor

@mirandakuligpoetry